An Actor in Training

By

Javaris Rhodie

© Copyright 2022 by Javaris Rhodie - All rights reserved.

It is not legal to reproduce, duplicate, or transmit any part of this document in either electronic means or printed format. Recording of this publication is strictly prohibited.

This book is dedicated to:

Dave Shalansky,

Daniel Daily,

Ray Virta,

Robert Manning Jr,

And America Barcenas De La Luz

Thank you all for giving me the necessary tools to succeed.

Thank you for teaching me about myself.

With admiration and respect.

-Javaris

Introduction

This book is not going to teach you how to be perfect and never mess up. It will give you the necessary tools you need to successfully navigate your way through your training. In this book I share experiences I had or witnessed while in conservatory training. Providing you with stories of both success and failure. I lay out plans, strategies and routines that will put you on the path to being an incredible student in your training. I am no professional coach or teacher with an extended list of credentials but what I do have is 2 years of experience at America's #1 ranked performing arts school with a vast knowledge of what is expected of someone in a performing arts program. The information in this book will transform you from a wide-eyed young student navigating training through trial and error to a young professional who every teacher will want to work with and every student will want to be. Not only have I used the information in this book for my benefit, but I have also helped a multitude of people who have come to me for advice on navigating the crazy world of performing arts training. These aren't all just personal tips that I have come up with on a whim but actual lessons I have learned from different teachers and working professionals during my time in conservatory. By purchasing this book, you are already one step ahead of everyone else, but that isn't all. You must not only read this book but take the lessons in it and apply them to your life. I promise after you put this down you will be 10 steps ahead of the game and a young professional ready to tackle anything your training will throw at you. Rather you know it or not, the first day you step into your training is the first day of your professional career as a performance artist. This book will help you navigate the new word you are about to enter. This book is for you. I want to see you succeed, do great things and blossom into the well-rounded professional actor that you have the potential to be. That all starts in your training, this book will aid you in that.

My Journey

Before we get started, I know you all be wondering who the hell am I and what am I about? Well...

My name is Javaris Rhodie I am an actor (and now I guess Author) based in New York City. I started my training in February of 2020, just a few months ahead of the Covid-19 shutdown (what a wonderful time to start college right!)

I trained at the American Musical And Dramatic Academy, also referred to as AMDA, on the New York City campus. I was born and raised in Elizabethtown, NC. Growing up I always knew I wanted to be an actor and that I was born to do better than what I saw in my hometown. Growing up in a small town in the south, wanting to be an actor is a far-fetched dream for some. When you tell people in a town like that you want to be an actor, they always give you that look, you know the look when their eyes get big and they plaster a fake smile on their face as they nod and go "Ohhh Okay, that's nice" I knew I had to leave eventually if I wanted to succeed. I always dreamed of being in New York City for some reason, I just remember seeing it on TV and in the movies and knowing that's where I belonged. So, I worked my ass off to get here. I knew that I wanted to go to college for acting, I knew that I had to have training, because anyone can have talent, but I knew I needed technique. I had only ever heard of Juilliard while growing up so naturally that was my dream school, but I knew that I needed other options, so I researched every performing arts school in New York, It was important to me that I went to a school that was specifically for performing arts, I didn't want to go to a big university that had a pretty good drama program or something of that nature. So, after finding my top choices I then went and read the curriculum for each school's program. I wanted to know what they were offering me that the others didn't I wanted to know what their training consisted of. I read everything word for word because that's how important it was to me. I finally narrowed my choices down to Juilliard, AMDA and AADA. The summer before my junior year in high school My grandfather took me on my first trip to New York, I was thrilled but instead of using this trip to sightsee and be a tourist I knew I had to use this opportunity to my advantage. Before we even hit the road, I had set up and open house and tour with each school. The first one I went to was AMDA, and I was overwhelmed with excitement and joy, seeing so many young performers doing what they love. Seeing the dancers run through the hall to get to their next class, hearing the singers in the rooms belting their hearts out, seeing the actors walk around in full costume with props, I knew I was where I belonged. After the presentation had wrapped up, I was informed that AMDA allowed high school Juniors to audition as well. Within the next 15 minutes I had my audition date set for that coming December, it all happened so fast and felt like a whirlwind. The moment I got back to North Carolina I picked out my audition materials and worked on them nonstop for four months leading up to my audition. I auditioned December 8th, 2018, and was accepted that following January, and my life was changed forever. Once I got to AMDA I realized that this was a world I felt connected to but one that was so foreign to me. I knew nothing. I didn't know a lot of the terms being used by those around me. I had no previous knowledge of how rehearsals went. I had no prior theatrical knowledge, so I went into it all bind. I didn't let that stop me from being the best version of myself possible. I worked hard to learn everything I could in my first few weeks. I wanted to feel as if I belonged. I tell you all this to say, I worked my ass off, did my homework and used every opportunity to make sure I got to where I wanted in life. That's the type of mindset and work ethic you need going into your training and this industry. This book will teach you how to do just that.

"Better Three hours too soon than a minute too late"
-William Shakespeare

Time Is Money

It's the age old saying that time is money, well in this case it isn't necessarily money, but one day, when you are a working professional in the industry, it will be, so get it together now. I know you may think this is going to be a drawn-out lecture on why you should always be early and never late and all that jazz, well… it is, but there are more valuable lessons here that will serve you well, it's a reason why it's first in the book

Early Is On Time, On Time Is Late, Late Should Never Be An Option

There are two types of people in training. There are those who are at least 15 minutes early to everything if they can control it, and there are those who think arriving by the start time, whether it be one minute before, is an accomplishment. If you fall into the latter category, you need to reevaluate some things. My very first day at AMDA they gave a huge speech on this exact topic, and the amount of people who let it go in one ear and out the other was staggering. It is important to set an example not only for those around you but for yourself, by always being as early as possible.

Nothing screams unprofessional more than someone who can't be on time. So, the trick to always being on time is to be early…. always. I used to hate seeing my peers stumble into class five to three minutes before class and seeing them rush to get themselves together, it was exhausting just looking at it. Don't be that person.

Being early not only gives you the professional edge over everyone else who isn't but it gives you a multitude of opportunities. You can get in the room and get a feel for the space you will be working in. A teacher of mine always used to say "piss in the corners" which means get a feel for every inch of the space you will be working in so that you can become familiar and comfortable with it. Being early allows you to prepare yourself for the scene, dance, song or whatever you are about to do in the following hours.

    A good way to ensure that you are on time (early) is to establish a routine. This routine can be weekly, daily or whatever caters to your schedule and your needs. The most important routine one should have is a morning routine. Have a routine you follow every morning that will not only get you warmed up and ready for your day but will prepare you for success and give you what you need to excel in class. This routine is what will determine the rest of your day and how well you perform. Don't be that kid strolling into the 8AM class looking groggy and tired because you just rolled out of bed, threw on something and haven't even had a sip of water. Be that professional performer who has a well-established morning routine that sets you up for success.

    I'm sure any college student in America could tell you that sleep is scarce during your studies. While in performing arts

An Actor In Training

training, though it may seem smart to prioritize sleep over an established morning routine... it's kind of not. Now I'm not saying you don't need sleep and that you should work yourself to the bone without rest, but what I am saying is, the luxurious amount of sleep you may be used to or what is considered to be the appropriate amount may not always be necessary. I have had nights where I slept only four or five hours but because of my morning routine, I was able to continue throughout the day without missing a beat, (and, not to toot my own horn but I don't drink coffee so imagine that) I can't give you a clear-cut picture of what your morning routine should look like because everyone has different needs and only you know your body, so do what works best for you. Again, I'm not telling you that you don't need sleep, because you absolutely do! Sleep is important and will do you well of course.

    Try including things that will warm you up physically such as stretches or a light workout. Include something to warm up and energize those raspy morning vocals. Give yourself time to think about the day ahead of you and what you'll need. Make sure you have your bag packed with everything you may need and more. Make sure you are putting nutrients into your body that will help jumpstart your day. Maybe even allow yourself time to chat with a friend before taking on the day, just to start your day off with some friendly conversation. Most importantly, HYDRATE!

"Tardiness and absences are the number one red flags in an actor, that tells me a lot about your professionalism and work ethic. A big part of being an actor is being on time or early, if you are consistently late, it will affect how your instructors and peers view you… another red flag is lack of preparation, you are not only letting your scene partner, peers, and instructor down, you're letting yourself down.

Those that succeed in their training are those that know how to manage their time and communicate.

You are going to work more as an actor in training than you will in a very long time, so take advantage of this opportunity… This is a time to fall on your face, don't worry about being perfect. Raise your standards, lower your expectations.

It goes remarkably far having a positive attitude. There are moments where a positive attitude is everything. Sometimes you have someone so Negative that it just brings everyone down, we all have bad days but that doesn't mean you can't show up with a positive attitude and good work ethic. If you are someone who has a bad attitude and takes everything personally, it makes it much more difficult to work with you in the school setting and that

An Actor In Training

can inevitably make an industry professional not want to work with you in the future.

Knowing who you are, even just a little bit can be extremely helpful, you are going to take a hard look at yourself once your training begins."

-Dave Shalansky

Actor/Director/Teacher

Dave's select TV credits include Recurring Guest Star on Grey's Anatomy, Guest Stars on Elementary, Famous in Love, Divorce (with Sarah Jessica Parker), HBO's Vinyl (with Ray Romano), The Mysteries of Laura (with Debra Messing), Nurse Jackie (with Edie Falco).

Half Hour

During my first week of my third semester at AMDA I had a teacher who used to always come in class and say, "in the professional theatre we have this thing called half hour". He would tell us that the time before half hour, was time that everyone got together and had coffee, talked, laughed and whatever else. When half hour was called everyone was preparing for the show, scene or whatever was about to be performed. During your training, it's always half hour. What I mean by that is, every moment not on stage or in front of a teacher, you should be preparing yourself for what's about to come. Which is another reason you should always arrive early.

I used to have a class at 8AM every Wednesday morning during my third semester. I always arrived no later than 7:15. Sometimes some of my peers had arrived a little early too, I would say good morning and the usual small talk for maybe five minutes, then I would go into the lobby area down the hall and read over my lines, read the full scene I was doing that day, read over my notes from the previous class or rehearsal. I was preparing myself, getting into the headspace that I needed to be in, focusing. Some of my peers decided to do the opposite. They would come in and bring loud talking, gossip, and whatever else didn't belong. I simply would remove myself from the environment to continue doing what I had to or put some headphones on to drown them out.

When a teacher walks in the room, they shouldn't find their students chatting, playing around and unfocused. My teacher used to always say "When I come in and hear everyone going over their lines instead of gossiping, I'll be happy."

Part of our daily preparation was a thorough

An Actor In Training

warmup that would get us grounded in our bodies and get our voice warmed up. A warmup is not just to get you ready for that class, it's to get you focused, in the proper headspace for what's about to happen. A warmup should be taken just as seriously as any of your other work. This is not a time to make unnecessary noise or comments, laugh and giggle or try to be a class clown. Not only will you look unprofessional if you do this, but like an ass as well, this time isn't just for you, it's for everyone, so if you are doing all those unnecessary antics, they can't focus and you're the one everyone wants to secretly hit.

An Actor In Training

In many of my classes the teacher had given us control over the warmups after the first few weeks and trusted that we would start on time and carry on the way we would as if they were in the room. Some people took advantage of this and decided it was okay to laugh and play during the warmup until the teacher came in. Well one day the teacher came in and none of us had realized. We were goofing around and not taking the warmup seriously. You can bet that he was not happy seeing his students be so unprofessional. I had never seen that specific teacher so frustrated and disappointed. We had broken his trust and after that incident he came to class right on the dot to make sure we were behaving during our warmups. My next semester the same thing happened, the teacher trusted us with the warmup routine, so he didn't have to monitor us. People tried to take advantage of this, but I had learned my lesson. I would be the one in the room quietly but sternly saying "quiet, we need to focus" or "why is everyone talking." Yea I got called out for being "bitchy" during the warmups, but I wasn't going to let the same thing happen to me again. More importantly I wasn't going to allow them to steal my focus and opportunity to truly warmup, and neither should you. That time is your time, you have the right to request respect while in the space and if your peers can't respect that, bring it up to the instructor privately and let them know what's going on. Reclaim your time!

Use Time Wisely

Once you are in your creative space/classroom, everything you do during that time should have some significance. After you're all warmed up and class has started, you need to be fully present and taking advantage of the time. Take notes, whether you are working or not, you can learn so much from observing your peers and hearing the notes they are receiving. If a word is said in class that you don't know, look it up or write it down to look up later (because I beg you to please not be on your phone during class). Be attentive, and for the love of Shakespeare please do not fall asleep, the ultimate sign of disrespect in any class.

While you are working, this time is the most valuable, use it diligently. When you are getting notes from a teacher, don't try to open a dialogue about what the thought process was behind everything (there are exceptions) take the note, go back to work and apply it, this way you are able to work more and receive more notes that can lead to the betterment of your performance, because if you spend too much time talking about one note (unnecessarily) you are limiting your time to work and receive new notes. You want to try and soak up everything you can during this time. When a teacher would give me a note, I would nod my head and say "okay" to let them know I understood and asked any necessary clarifying questions, so that way I could immediately apply them and work towards a forward progression until another note was needed. If you are ever confused or unsure about a note, please let it be known, you will not be penalized for asking "can you elaborate on that note" or simply saying "I'm sorry but I don't understand what you mean by that can you explain further". It's better to take a little extra time trying to understand a note rather than wasting time doing something half assed because you didn't understand or making them stop the performance to give you the same note because you didn't get it the first time. They are there to help you but it's up to you to ask for it.

During the time in between, such as breaks or transitions from one scene to the next, this is not a time to start talking and playing. This is a time to prepare for what's next, give you an opportunity to run to the restroom, grab water or get up and stretch a little so you can stay warmed up if you haven't worked yet. If you are the one up to work and the break isn't quite over yet, don't waste that. Use that time to ground yourself in the space, connect with your scene partners, run lines, do whatever to prepare yourself. If you aren't up to work, do not distract those that are by trying to play with them, they have work to do and don't need you taking away their focus. Sit there and observe, read over your notes.

    I remember I was doing a scene from Hamlet once, the scene between Hamlet and Ophelia, which takes place right after the famous "To Be, or not the be" speech. This meant I had to have a certain energy coming into the scene and at the time I hadn't mastered how to do that without a great deal of physical movement. When the teacher called for a five-minute break and announced that my scene was up next, I spent three of those minutes hydrating, connecting with my scene partner and moving around the space, the next two minutes I spent doing the fastest jumping jacks I could manage, per my teachers request. When the scene started, I had the necessary breath and energy that the teacher requested for the scene. After the first week I didn't have to do jumping jacks or extreme exercise to get my breathe and energy up, I had learned how to get there on my own, which was the goal.

Javaris Tip #1
Don't Complain

Like in almost every profession, complaining is not appreciated. If your class runs late and you're ready to go home, if you had to wake up early for an 8 AM class and you aren't a morning person, if you have 6 classes back to back with no big breaks in between, If You have been in rehearsal for hours and are ready to go...Complaining is a NO NO! it is unprofessional and just downright annoying. You aren't the only one having to stay late or wake up early and work hard, so if you are complaining people will slowly dislike you and not want to work with you.

Javaris Tip #2
No Yawning

I learned very early on during my time at AMDA that yawning was also a big no no.
Yawning is frowned upon in most performing art programs because it gives the impression that you are tired, bored, uninterested, and not present.
A teacher of mine told me during my third semester that if we ever yawned in a professional Rehearsal, he would haunt us in his after life because he had taught us better.

Yawning is overall a no go. I know it may be hard at first but whatever you do, please don't

An Actor In Training

yawn, and if you can't control it, learn to play it off well, sometimes when I really had to let one out and couldn't control it, I would pretend as if I was massaging my jaw to stay warmed up, this was extremely beneficial since I got to let out a good (noiseless) yawn and warm myself back up during class.

"We Will Meet; and there we may rehearse most obscenely and courageously"

-William Shakespeare

Rehearsal

Rehearsal is a very important aspect of your craft, learning how to navigate a rehearsal process during your training will help you in the long run. With a bulk of your time being spent in rehearsal - sometimes without a teacher or director present- it's imperative to know how one should behave, work and think while in the rehearsal process.

It Is Necessary

There are some people who try to skate by and think they can avoid rehearsals but not only are they wrong they are out of their mind. Would you expect to be a part of a professional production and not rehearse? Whether it's a scene for class, a monologue, song, or solo dance, get to rehearsing! The rehearsal process allows you to make discoveries about your piece that you may not have made on your own by just going over it in your mind. You can run through the piece multiple times in a space, giving your mind a chance to analyze it in a different way. You can see the blocking which can add to whatever you have been working on.

    During my second semester at AMDA, I had the opportunity to work on a scene from "Spike Heels" by Theresa Rebeck with a good friend of mine. At AMDA you are expected to put in three to six hours of rehearsal outside of class, depending on how many times the class met during the week. My scene partner and I thought we could get away with one rehearsal, so one hour a week when this class required a full six. We thought we had a handle on the scene, we did all our character analysis work and had read the play over several times and thought we had it in

An Actor In Training

the bag. Well, one day we presented in front of our teacher, and it was horrible, to the point the teachers only note was "this looks unrehearsed". It was embarrassing and humbling. After falling on our ass in front of the entire class, my scene partner and I got in rehearsals for all hours that were required of us, it wasn't an easy process, it was tedious and hard but *necessary*. We kept discovering things in each rehearsal that we never would have thought of if we kept the same lazy 1 hour a week process, we had been doing. The next week we went in and presented the scene after putting in the *NECESSARY* rehearsal time. It felt incredible, we were much more confident in the work, and it showed. Once the scene ended, we looked at our teacher for feedback and he looked at the both of us and gave us "jazz hands" which was a big deal for this teacher, the first thing that came out of his mouth was "I can tell you boys have been in rehearsal, keep it up, it's paying off"

It may be a pain in the ass sometimes but putting in a good amount of time is not only necessary but beneficial to your scene or whatever you are working on. Don't let rehearsal become optional, it should always be obligatory in your process.

The Do's and Don'ts's

Rehearsals are not a time to goof around or sit and talk about the amazing show you saw last night with your friends. It's a time to work. Without a teacher/director being present in some rehearsals for pieces that may be presented in class, some people can become a bit distracted and waste time that could be used for the betterment of the piece.

Having a scene with friends or people you enjoy talking to can sometimes be challenging because you naturally want to chat with them, but this is still a dedicated time for work. Not saying that side conversations that are relevant can't occur but it's important to keep them at a minimum and stay focused on the work at hand. If you want to have time to chat and go through thoughts & just talk about the work, schedule time for that in your rehearsal so you can stay on track.

Rehearsals should be treated just like a class setting, everyone should be on their best behavior, displaying proper theatre etiquette. Working diligently on the scene. No one should be doing anything they wouldn't do in a professional rehearsal. Below are the basic dos and don'ts of a self-governed rehearsal:

DO'S:

- Be explorative and try things out, no one is going to see it

- Be open minded. Take into consideration any ideas from your scene partners

- Take timed breaks. Rehearsals can be challenging

- Rehearse it full out. Not being on voice, or not performing an action full out can be a huge disservice.

- Rehearse with props/proper blocking. You don't want to be thrown off during the performance or presentation because you neglected to go through blocking or utilize props.

- Take nots. Noting your rehearsals and what was done can be beneficial in future rehearsals.

DON'T:

- Sit around chatting for an hour about irrelevant topics

- Treat it like a chore. Your scene partners shouldn't get the feeling you don't want to be there

- Complain.... We've been over this one..

- Ask "are we done yet" it sends a horrible message that you want to leave and don't care about the progression of the scene

- Direct your scene partners… this should be a given, but you'd be surprised how many rehearsals I've been in where a scene partner thinks they are now the director.

- Make comments on another actor's performance… it is not your job to determine whether someone is good or bad, it's your job to do your best for the betterment of the scene.

The list can go on for days, but these are just come of the basics to keep in mind when entering a rehearsal process. Some may seem small but trust me, they make a difference.

Appearance

Your Rehearsal can be impacted by what you choose to wear. You want to make sure that you're prepared to work without being restricted by any clothing, jewelry, hair, or an uncomfortable choice of shoes.

If you are rehearsing for a specific scene, any professional will tell you it is wise to rehearse in the shoes of your character. You don't want your performance to be altered when you get on stage in your 6-inch heels for the character and you've been rehearsing in Crocs and flip flops. (I really hope none of you ever show up to rehearsal in flip flops… unless of course it's for the character)

Rehearsals can also be very long and sometimes tedious. You don't want to be stuck in an all-day rehearsal in an uncomfortable outfit. Let me break it down.

What to Wear:

- **Moveable clothing**
- **Comfortable shoes (or the shoes of your character)**
- **Hair up and out of face**
- **A smile**

What NOT to wear:

- **Skinny Jeans…Or jeans period**
- **Jewelry (that is not a part of the scene)**
- **Too much perfume**

- **A Frown**

- **…..Flip Flops**

You notice Jewelry is on the list of what not to wear. Although we all love a statement piece and shiny rings, they are not for the rehearsal process. You need to be a blank canvas, if not in your characters wardrobe. I remember a teacher of mine once saying "What's the point of coming to a conservatory if you are unwilling to ditch the jewelry for a few hours during rehearsal"

Altering your appearance in the middle of rehearsal or the middle of the semester may not go over so well with your teacher/Director. Especially if they have cast you in a particular role. Although it is amazing to be able to assert our individuality with things such as piercing, tattoos, hair etc. It is always wise to speak to the teacher/director first, just as you would in a professional production.

    I remember a friend of mine decided to get his ears pierced in the middle of the semester one weekend. The following Monday we went into rehearsals for our final scenes we were set to present at the end of the semester. Our teacher asks him to take out his earrings before the scene, but he was unable to do so because the piercings were new and could not be taken out within a certain time span. Well as you can imagine that did not go over well with the teacher, so much so that he pulled my friend to the side and lectured him on the importance of not doing something like that in the middle of a rehearsal process.

Your personal appearance during rehearsal is not to be taken lightly it can really affect the entire process. You don't have to be dressed to impress but you do have to be dressed for success. I used to wear a black tank top, black joggers, and whatever shoes I had for the character to every single rehearsal. I hope you find that comfortable rehearsal attire that will ultimately lead you to a successful rehearsal.

Be Prepared

As I've stated before, rehearsals can sometimes be long and tedious, you want to make sure you are prepared for any and everything that may occur during the process. Be prepared to do the necessary work. Trust me, you don't want to be the person who doesn't have a pen to take notes with, or the person who didn't bring any water to the first day of Tech.

I had a teacher once who said, once the class began, if you weren't up on your feet working, a notebook should be open. On your lap with a pen ready in your hand.

The following list will suit you up with everything you will need to bring to ensure you are prepared for a successful rehearsal. The list contains both literal & figurative contents.

What To Bring (literally)

- **The material (Script, Sheet Music, Choreography notes)**
- **Notebook**
- **Pen, Pencils, highlighters**
- **Water**
- **Snacks**

An Actor In Training

- **Notes from class / last rehearsal**

What To Bring (Figuratively)

- **A Smile**
- **A Good attitude**
- **Good work ethic**
- **An Open mind**
- **A mind full of ideas**
- **The same passion that made you want to pursue this in the first place.**

Preparedness can be what sets you apart from the rest, in

both a good and bad way. It can be the deciding factor for someone wanting to work with you or not. It can tell a teacher/director more about you than you could ever say out of your mouth. Being prepared is a basic skill one must acquire in life, especially in the performing arts.

During my third semester at AMDA, I was fortunate enough to have one of the most well-known teachers at the school. He was known for being an extraordinary teacher with a no BS policy. It was the first day of class and we were all eager to get started on our first scenes, he told everyone to take out a notebook and something to write with.

An Actor In Training

Everyone except one girl in the class did so, it was like in the movies when all the heads turn at once to one person. She explained she didn't bring a notebook or anything to write with and that she was going to take notes on her phone. The silence was deafening. You could see just how annoyed the teacher was… and that was her first impression. He let her off the hook since it was the first class but explained if it ever happened again, she would have to leave class for the day. He went on to tell everyone in the class, when any work is being done in class you should have a notebook and pen out taking notes, even if they are not directly to you. We learn a lot from watching others.

    Now it's easy for me to sit here and act as if I never had any slips ups. Of course I did, I am human. During my fourth semester, I had one of the biggest slip ups in my entire AMDA career. We were set to pitch plays for our final showcase. We had a few meetings before to discuss what we needed to have prepared for that evening. The day before I spent all day getting all my pitches together, I had all my scenes printed out and stapled, there was a copy for everyone who I planned on reading with, a copy for both directors, the stage manager, and a spare.

On my way to pitch night, my water spilled all in my bag and got everything wet and my papers were destroyed. I had to think quick. I hopped on the subway train to the nearest staples store to try and get everything together again (with very little time to do so) I was only able to get a few copies done before the printer ran out of ink and an associate had to come assist…. Just my luck. Time was not on my side this day, neither was the MTA. I took what papers I had and shoved them in my bag and booked it back to the studio where pitches were taking place

An Actor In Training

(Without being late, because late is NEVER an option).

When it came time for me to pitch, I realized that all my scripts were out of the place, and nothing had been stapled and they were all over the place. I stood there like a bumbling idiot trying to find the last page to one of the scenes to hand to the director and after about a minute he lectured be for being ill-prepared and explained how this could cost me a job in the real world. Now I could have tried to explain my day and all that was going on, but they would have been nothing but excuses and would not change the fact I was ill-prepared. Once we went on our 10-minute break I went to the bathroom and cried my eyes out because I had just screwed up big time on the first night of pitches for final showcase, in front of two directors I respected and admired immensely.

    Although I knew the events of that day did not define my work ethic or me as a professional, and I couldn't help some of the events that took place. I was still disappointed in myself, but I wasn't going to let it break me, and I damn sure wasn't going to let the directors think of me as an ill prepared unprofessional. I sent both directors and the stage manager an apology emails that same night, and from that day forward

An Actor In Training

I was always on top of things and was prepared for everything. Anything I needed to print out, I printed an extra of just in case and stored it in a folder in a separate compartment away from my water bottle.

    As you can see, preparedness can either make you or break you during your training, it makes an impression on not only the teachers and directors but your peers, and it will for the rest of your career. I hope you have already made preparedness a basic skill in your wheelhouse and if not, do so now.

"Keep an open mind, the most debilitating thing I see in students is when they come in believing they already know something. In this industry there are so many right answers, there's not one way to do it, if you come in thinking you have a leg up, you are not going to benefit from the program.

There's a hunger in some students that drives everything, it drives their curiosity and their work ethic. The students that tend to succeed in my class are the ones that are hungry to learn.

If you truly don't know what your rehearsal is supposed to look like, communicate that to your instructor… Always have schedule for rehearsals go into it with a plan. Maybe set aside 15 minutes to talk through ideas and notes then dedicate 10 minutes to go through beats, then 30 minutes to rehearse it on your feet etc..... Rehearsals are the ideal time to fall on your face, fail and try something else.

We know when you're not prepared, we can tell, no matter how good you are at flying by the seat of your pants. If you come in unprepared, there's only so far I can take you, there's only so far you can go with your scene partner(s) but if you come prepared and having done the work, there's no limit to where we can go and how deep we can dig.

An Actor In Training

I love watching students fall in love with acting."

- Suzy Jane Hunt
Actor/Teacher

Suzy Jane Hunt is an actress, research artist, and educator; an acting teacher at the Academy of Music and Dramatic Arts (AMDA); an adjunct professor at NYU Steinhardt's program in Educational Theatre; and a creative collaborator with the Verbatim Performance Lab.

Acting credits include Dear Evan Hansen, Dead Accounts on Broadway, Viola in Twelfth Night at the Stratford Festival, Alice on FX's The Americans, Agent Schiffman on CBS's Person of Interest, The Good Wife, Blindspot, Elementary. suzyjanehunt.com

Javaris Tip #3
Get A Good Bag, And Use it

A good bag is essential to any college student but especially to us performers. We need something that can hold all our regular class materials and then some (for those days we may have an extra rehearsal). It must be durable, reliable and if possible, stylish.

Here are some essentials that every performing arts student should have in their bag

- *Water (Always stay Hydrate!)*
- *Script (even if you are off book, always have a copy on you)*

An Actor In Training

- *Journal*
- *Writing tools*
- *Charger / Portable charger*
- *Snacks*
- *Face Towel (in case you get too sweaty during class or rehearsal)*
- *Deodorant*
- *Breath Mints (don't be in someone's face speaking on voice, with stink breath)*
- *An extra Plain T-Shirt (Anything can happen, trust me)*
- *A Book (perhaps one from the recommended reading list)*

Javaris Tip #4
Conservatory Couture

When in a performing arts program, what you wear is a vital part of your training, it can either enhance your performance or restrict it. During my time at AMDA, I learned a few tips & Tricks when it came to dressing for success.

Always where a nice fitting top and lose fitting pants that will allow you to move without any restriction. I usually went with a nice black tank top and pair of quality joggers

Don't' wear anything too loud in color or distracting, for

the obvious reason that it can distract both the audience and your scene partner and take away from the work you are doing.

Try to wear something that will allow you to be very neutral, something like all black or neutral colors that will allow the teacher/director to see you as the character before the costumes come in to play.

"Striving for success without hard work is like trying to harvest where you haven't planted."
— David Bly

Work Ethic

Work Ethic is important during any college program, but it is crucial in a performing arts program. Your work ethic will speak for itself. Everyone can assess you by that alone, including teachers and directors. Your work ethic can sometimes be the deciding factor of you being given a certain role or not. It's important to develop good work ethic during your first semester/year so that it continues throughout your training.

An Actor In Training

Teachers see a lot of students every year come and go, all talented in their own ways, but the ones with the best work ethic are the ones that usually stand out.

    During my time at AMDA I became well known for my work ethic. I was admired by most peers, even some of my teachers took notice and recognized me for having both a great work ethic and an amazing attitude every single day. My friend Jon likes to say I'm the hardest working person he knows (his words not mine). For some, work ethic comes naturally, others must work to develop it. I was lucky enough to be one of the ones it came naturally to, however throughout my training, I helped friends and peers develop a good work ethic.

Work Ethic Becomes you

It's no secret that performing arts programs are rigorous and sometimes very fast pace. During your time in training, you will need to develop a work ethic that will not only help you survive and get by but one that will make you stand out from the rest. Having a good work ethic can be what a lot of people remember you by, including teachers who could potentially get you a gig post-graduation. Everyone has different work ethics; you will meet some people who are some of the hardest working individuals you know, and you'll meet others who just simply don't care enough to develop a good work ethic.

Think about it, you are going to enter an industry where you will be performing 8 shows a week, or filming for 16 hours sometimes. So, during your training is the perfect place to start developing a good work ethic. I know at this point you may be asking "How do I do that?" Well, I'm not going to lie, it isn't easy. I think work ethic revolves around three big pillars; those pillars are:

1. Dedication

2. Focus

3. Sacrifice

Keeping these three pillars in mind will always lead to an incredible work ethic, but first let's elaborate on them.

Dedication: You must be completely dedicated to your training. Soaking up every single lecture, note, and regular conversation. I mean, why pay all this money to not be dedicated? Dedicate yourself to putting in extra hours in rehearsal, dedicate yourself to being early, when possible,

These exact three pillars are what kept me on the path of having a work ethic that stood out from many. Take them and use them for yourself to create that work ethic that will have teachers speaking nothing but great things about you in the teachers' lounge (because trust me, they do talk).

Learn To Love The Process

The sooner you learn to love the process, the easier work ethic will come to you. I completely understand how jarring it can be when first entering a performing arts program. You want to do

An Actor In Training

everything right, you feel the need to "prove" yourself, you are overwhelmed. These things are what lead to many people falling behind and developing bad habits that ultimately lead to a horrible work ethic.

When I say learn to love the process, what I mean is you must learn to fall in love with literally everything. Love going to late night rehearsals, love having 8AM classes, love having to learn lines within a matter of minutes. Because this time is precious, you don't know the next time you are going to be this booked and busy as an artist. You literally get to do what you love every single day, although at times the workload can seem a bit much, never forget why you started. The love and passion you have that made you choose this program should always be in the forefront.

I remember during a class where we had been rehearsing our final scenes for almost a month at this point and everyone looked like they were almost on their last leg when the teacher said something that perked everyone up, he said "Remember when acting was fun". We all laughed because we had realized how much fun it is under all the hard work and long hours, we put in.

Never let anyone or anything take away the love and passion you have for your craft, even when the going gets tough, remember why you chose this career, and I promise it will sooth your soul.

Find The Balance

When developing a killer work ethic, you can sometimes go overboard and overwork yourself, which is just as bad as a poor work ethic. When you overwork yourself no one wins. You are going to feel fatigued, mentally tired, and unfocused. Everyone around will feel it as well, you are going to lack in energy, you may be absent in conversation and sometimes you can even look like you are overworked.

    I remember during my second semester at AMDA I became so obsessed with the idea of working harder, putting in more hours and being laser focused. Now that may not sound like a bad idea, however it led to me overworking myself because I didn't take time for me, time to rest, I didn't even take time to have a light lunch with friends. One day in class while I was packing up my teacher at the time approached me and said that I looked like I was simply exhausted. I had explained to him that I had been working around

An Actor In Training

the clock every day of the week. He sat me down and told me that although it's important to put in hard work and have a good work ethic, I was human and needed rest. He said that it was okay to take a break sometimes and not overwork myself, that I had to find the balance for myself. I remember leaving that conversation and crying my entire walk back to the dorm, mostly because I was so tired on the inside and felt defeated, but also because it meant so much to me to have someone actually see me and care enough to have a simple conversation with me that changed everything for me. I'm lucky enough to call that teacher a friend today, I will forever be grateful for that conversation Dave.

I want you to know too, that it's okay to take a rest and to not overwork yourself or your scenes. The balance is going to be different for everyone but please find one for yourself. It's going to be hard at first, but you will get the hang of it. If you have all your homework done, you know all your lines and you have some spare time on a Friday night, go have a good time with your friends, it's not going to hurt, if anything it's going to help.

We can get so caught up in all the work that sometimes we

lose ourselves, we lose the light inside of us. Don't let that happen, always listen to your body, your mind, and your heart. Don't push yourself beyond your limits, now don't mistake that with not challenging yourself every now and then. And when it's all said and done, just please be kind to yourself.

An Actor In Training

"You must constantly absorb everything around you. Come here ready to be serious and curious, serious about your work and curious about everything to do with it.

Hard Work looks effortless, no one see's the 100'000 hours an actor puts in before showtime…Not everyone should be an actor, it has less to do with talent and more to do with persistence… Many students end up dropping out because they realize they must self-generate and be resilient, both of those things require an incredible amount of patience and ability to see the road ahead.

An Actor In Training

The most successful students are those that fall and get right back up, they have resilience. They aren't afraid to make mistakes. You should make many mistakes but never make the same mistake twice.

In training and in this industry, you must weather the storm and for some, weathering the storm isn't as nice as being dry throughout life"

-Ray Virta

Actor/Director/Teacher

Ray has 40 years of teaching experience including AMDA, NYU/PHTS

An Actor In Training

Ray was awarded the 2002 St. Clair Bayfield Award for Outstanding Shakespeare Performance in the metropolitan NYC area for his work as Benedick in Much Ado About Nothing at The Pearl. Broadway: Therese Raquin, An Enemy of the People, Arcadia, Hedda Gabler, A Man for All Seasons, Boeing-Boeing, Naked Girl on the Appian Way, Democracy, Betrayal, The Real Thing, The School for Scandal, Inherit the Wind. Off-Broadway: 19 shows including Glimmer, Glimmer and Shine, Eyes for Consuela (MTC), Langella's Cyrano (Roundabout); Resident-Pearl Theatre. National Tours: M. Butterfly; The Acting Company. Regional: Over 40 lead/featured roles including Romeo, Macbeth, Torvald, Orsino, Berowne.

Directing: Comedie of Errors (Brooklyn College), The Way of the World (Pearl), As You Like It (KCSC). Reading: Just South of Paradise by Charlotte Wooden.

JavarisTip #5
Read The Syllabus

The Syllabus is often skipped at any school; however, it can be very beneficial to read.

Some teachers will put a full breakdown of the course and be very detailed with their syllabus while others may not have much to go from, it's always worth peeking at the syllabus to try and gauge how the class will go.

There is usually a recommended reading list somewhere in the syllabus (sometimes along with a required reading list). I always say make the recommended reading your required reading. Any books, plays or reading material that may be recommended to you for that course, are recommended for a reason, that most likely means that the teacher uses those materials for reference throughout the semester. Plus, it never hurts to read an extra book or two to educate yourself and grow as a performer.

An Actor In Training

Javaris Tip #6

Always Have One More time in you.

You always must have "one more time" in you. You must be willing to rehearse a scene over and over if necessary. You must be willing to go one more time every time it's asked of you.

My dance teacher first semester used to always have us run our dance "one more time" at the end of class… sometimes that "one more time" turned into four more times and we had to do the work.

> *Wise men speak because they have something to say; fools speak because they have to say something*
>
> -Plato

Communication

During your training, you will quickly come to realize just how important communication is. You will be working with people who have different personalities, different teachers who have different teaching style and at some points, with industry professionals. Communication skills develop as we grow and learn, you won't have all the proper communications tools right from the start. It will take time. This will give you the foundations for good communication while in training.

Effective & Appropriate Communication

You must be willing to communicate your feeling and needs to your instructors. No one can help you if you don't say anything, if you are feeling stuck or you don't understand something please speak up so you can get the necessary clarity for you to move forward. Your peers also deserve good communication from you. You need to communicate if you are going to be late to a rehearsal or class, if you need extra time in rehearsal, if something is going on that may affect the scene. You owe it to everyone around you to communicate clearly.

    Dealing with multiple personalities & different teaching styles can be challenging, if not done properly it can lead to petty arguments and cause tension within the group/cast which is never good for the work. Effectively and appropriately communicating your ideas and feelings will save you from a negative impact on the work.

    Everything should be discussed in a respectful manner. You must be willing to listen to others. Allowing others to share and contribute to discussions will let them know you respect what they have to say and are open to compromise. You can't have your way of thinking and expect everyone to go by what you want all the time. Everything is a group effort, and no one should feel as if their voice isn't being heard or that their thoughts and feelings don't matter.

Whenever disagreements arise, which they will... trust me, you should never begin to get out of character and/or raise your voice. Everyone should be able to discuss their point of view in a civil manner that will lead to an ultimate solution. Yelling and Childish behavior will get you nowhere, except labeled as "difficult to work with". No two people are going to always agree on everything, and that's okay. You don't always have to be right; you don't always have to prove your point. It's perfectly normal to have disagreements but how you deal with them will speak volumes about your character.

    Never and I mean NEVER get out of line with a teacher/director. I shouldn't have to say this, but I've seen it on several occasions during my training and each time it never ends well for the student. If you have something that you need to discuss with a teacher/director, there are ways to go about it.

An Actor In Training

You should never raise your voice at them or attempt to challenge their authority in front of your peers.

During my third (and toughest) semester at AMDA, our teacher assigned us the famous "O' for a muse of fire" monologue from "Henry V" by William Shakespeare. He gave it to us at 8 Pm that night and told us to have it fully memorized by 8Am the next day which is when our class met again. So that's 34 lines of Shakespeare to be memorized in roughly 12 hours. You only had one shot, if you missed even just one line or paused for too long, you got an F for that day and had to sit down…. Only one person passed

An Actor In Training

that day, everyone else earned an F for the day and got told to sit... including me. I know that sounds brutal however it was the best lesson I've learned in my life. He told us to raise our hands if we really felt we had it but the pressure got to us, I was the only one who raised my hand. He said that was only a glimpse into how much pressure you can feel in an audition room or on stage in a packed theater, he assured me I had done nothing wrong, but I can't let my nerves get the best of me to where I can't deliver. He then asked everyone to raise their hand if they knew they didn't have it when they went to sleep last night, everyone else raised their hand. He then went on to say, "If you know you didn't have it why did you sleep?" Before he had the opportunity to finish speaking someone in the class jumped up out of their seat and said "THAT'S RIDICULOUS, HOW COULD YOU ASK THAT QUESTION?! YOU HAVE TO HAVE SLEEP FOR MEMORIZATION CRYSTALS TO FORM" She went on and on doing nothing but embarrassing herself. The teacher let her finish and calmy began to finish his original statement. He said, "Why did you allow yourself to sleep, imagine if this was your dream role and you only had one shot, you would stay up all night if you had to." He went on to explain he understood it was a very large and ridiculous demand and that it most likely would never be asked of us ever again.

Loose lips sink ships and can ruin your career

We are in an industry where everyone knows everyone, and one where your reputation is crucial. You must be careful of what you say and who you say it around. You don't want to be the person in the cast bad mouthing the director, because what if it gets back to him, or what if one of your cast mates is on the casting team for a project you go in to audition for?

No one wants to work with someone who is going to bad mouth their cast mates and/or director. There are certain things that should not be said while around your peers & cast mates. This not only leaves a negative impression, but it could also cost you in the long run.

A dear teacher of mine and actor by the name of Robert Manning Jr. always told me how important it was to watch my mouth in this industry. What to say, what not to say, when to say it and who to say it or not say it around. He told me that word of mouth spreads quicker than we think it may and to keep negative thoughts and opinions to ourselves because they could cost us a job one day.

During my final semester at AMDA we were given the wonderful opportunity to shoot a short film project that was a part of our finals, giving us footage for our reel post-graduation. there was someone who always had a bad attitude when working with a certain director. He decided he didn't like his directing style or how some of his footage was shot. Which is valid however instead of expressing this to the director in a respectful manner, he decided to bad mouth the director behind his back that night as he was working on another shot with other actors. It was completely unprofessional, and we all just tried to ignore him. He then went on to attack him personally making comments about him that had nothing to do with him as a director. Which is when I intervened because I happened to be very fond of the director, I told him that everyone was working hard, and no one deserved to be disrespected like that and perhaps he should keep those comments to himself. The same guy decided that on the last day of school he was going to continue to bad mouth this director again for absolutely no reason, considering he wasn't present. It started to infuriate my friends and me so much that we decided to gather our belongings and leave the room. We were not going to sit around such negativity and listen to someone be so disrespectful to someone we admired. Although he may not know it, the joke is on him, other teachers and directors took note of his bad attitude and bad-mouthing habits and sent notes of that along to casting directors they knew when asked about him.

An Actor In Training

Javaris Tip #7
Make a friend in the bookstore clerk

As young performers in training, we are always sourcing new material, which means we spend a good amount of time at the local bookstores. Having a friend in the clerk doesn't hurt. I have had so many conversations with bookstore clerks that turn into great friendships. It can be very beneficial to establish a great relationship with the bookstore clerk because they can help you when you need new material. I'm sure any clerk would be happy to help you find material if you simply ask, however when you create a relationship with them, they know you a little better and are able to help you on a deeper level. Also, it's nice to just show them some appreciation for all their hard work.

You get out what you put in

Many people expect their training to do all the work, that your school is going to teach you how to be the best actor, singer, or dancer the world has ever seen. They think just because they got into the school that its's going to be smooth sailing from there. That's when the hard work begins. Your school will give you all the tools to grow artistically and better yourself however it is up to you to put in the necessary work both in and out of class. You must hold yourself accountable, because at the end of the day no one else is. No one is going to hold your hand and make sure you are doing everything you can to grow. Although you may have friends, peers and even teachers who offer a helping hand every now and then, it's all on you.

    I encountered so many people who thought they would be able to party it up while in training and not face the reproductions. While there is nothing wrong with socialization and having fun with friends and peers. You can't expect to do it all the time and disregard your training. If you are deciding to go out and drink, smoke, and party every single night, it is not only going to take a toll on you but your work. As performing artists our body & voice are our instruments and we can't afford to mistreat them while training, or ever.

You can sit there and pout about your scene not getting good notes or say that the material was too difficult or blame your scene partner. When really it all starts and end with you. Instead of pouting about bad notes, use them to better the scene and fuel your growth.

Instead of saying the material was too difficult, work relentlessly to understand the material and what it's demanding of you. You have the power to change every single negative into a positive if you PUT IN THE WORK. If this was easy, everyone would be doing it.

I want you to look at your favorite actor, singer, dancer, performer of any kind. I want you to watch and read some of their interviews. While you look at these interviews, I want you to note one time they said it's easy. I want you to note one time they said they just slacked off and didn't put in great amount of work.

An Actor In Training

"When I started my training, I wish I would have known how fabulous I already was. It took me forever to develop my confidence and feel like I belonged there. You may be talented but if you don't believe that you are, other people won't believe it. You must own it and be confident. Be yourself and know that you are enough.

Know that you can learn from everyone around you. My classmates taught me so much about being a young adult in a different country. I moved from Mexico and English was my second language so there were culture differences that I had to ask help on understanding. You must be open to asking for advice, asking questions, and asking for help if you need it. You may feel the questions are stupid in your head and are afraid to ask it sometimes, but you look even worse when you don't ask

Kindness & work ethic in my students equals success to me. I will not remember if someone was able to do a triple pirouette or not, but I will remember kindness. In the end, your teacher, directors, choreographers etc. are people as well and want to work with kind, fun human beings who are willing to put in the work

If you are not ready to work hard, do not come. People

An Actor In Training

think because they don't like traditional studies that this will be a piece of cake. If you don't have work ethic and don't want to work hard for anything. This isn't going to work for you. You're going to sweat, cry and want to quit sometimes. It's going to hurt at times. It's just like any other job; you must invest a lot and do the necessary work."

-America Barcenas De La Luz
Actress/singer/choreographer/educator

Her credits include the role of 'Pepe' in Too Many Girls, 'Delee' in Smokey Joe's Cafe, Hairspray, Kiss Me Kate, Porgy & Bess (International tour), Bizet's Opera Carmen, among others. She toured throughout South America as a member of "Mexico Folklorico". For "Backbeard

An Actor In Training

the Musical" for NYMF 2017 she was the Associate Choreographer. America has over 10 years of experience teaching in Mexico and the USA and travels as a Ballet Guest teacher around the country.

> *"Adaptability is not imitation. It means power of resistance and assimilation"*
>
> **-Mahatma Gandhi**

Adjusting To A New Environment

Let me be the first person to tell you that it can be scary at first when entering your training. You must adjust to a new environment with brand new people and most likely you will be leaving your hometown and have to adjust to a new city. Imagine coming from a small rural town in North Carolina to Great big New York City, with no friends or family there to hold your hand, yea that was me.

An Actor In Training

You have two choices; you can let it get the best of you and stop you from living up to your potential or you can dive in headfirst. Luckily for me there were orientation activities that allowed everyone to become acquainted before classes started, giving us an opportunity to talk to everyone and get to know them before the madness began. I hope you have the same opportunity.

It's imperative that you become familiar with your surroundings. This is going to be your new home for a while rather you are doing a 4-year bachelor program, or a 2-year accelerated conservatory program, or even just a few weeks in an intensive.

Know the route from your dorms or apartment to all your class buildings, how long they take and if they are walkable when carrying costumes, props, etc. Know which areas to avoid and are not so safe at night for those times you have late night rehearsals. (I always recommend traveling with a buddy at night regardless). Know what food spots you are around in case you need a quick bite to eat on the way home. Know where the nearest urgent care and emergency room is. You really don't know how much you need to know about a new area until you are there and have no idea where anything is besides the nearest pizza joint.

Get your crew

Everyone has that group of people they are closer with than anyone else. They are especially important during this time in your life. They will be your friends, supporters, encouragers and even a shoulder to cry on when the going gets thought (which it will) Sometimes your crew may be just two people or one very great one. Just make sure when you find your crew, it's filled with people who are going to help you in the long run and not hinder you.

I was lucky enough to find one of my greatest friends and

inspirations during my first semester at AMDA. My great friend Jada Robinson. She not only was my best friend at the time but my biggest encourager, Jada pushed me like no other friend had before. I've always prided myself on my work ethic, but I learned so much from Jada during our first semester. She would drag me to the rehearsal rooms at 9PM to go over our dances we learned that week when I thought I already had it down. She would make me sit down and go over our voice & speech assignment when I would get too chatty with everyone in the dorm kitchen. When the rehearsal studios were all booked up and it looked like we had no options, Jada would make us rehearse a dance on the New York sidewalks or come to my tiny dorm room to go over lines for a scene. This girl was relentless in her pursuit to learn, grow and be better than we were before, and it bled onto me.

When the Covid-19 Pandemic hit and we all had to return to our homes with an uncertain future lingering over our heads, Jada and I texted and called each other every day, keeping each other's spirits up during the stressful transition to online instruction. Even when we had to switch to remote learning, Jada kept the same work ethic and I was right there with her, committing myself to the work regardless of the circumstances.

I beg all of you to please find your Jada, Encourage and love each other. It will make the biggest difference in your experience. I'm sure I would have done just fine if I hadn't met Jada, but we all need that someone in our corner who is going to push us from 100% to 150%.

After Covid restrictions eased a bit and we were allowed back on campus for in person instruction, Jada did not return right away so I had to make sure I found a crew who would be what Jada and I had been for each other. That fall I met my very best friends Jon, Cody, and Krista. Of course, I had other friends during this time who were encouraging, and I willingly surrounded myself with, but those three were my rocks. We all became incredibly close over that semester, so much so that we were each other's go to for scene partners if we had the opportunity to choose. Just because we were all friends that never affected the work, we still treated every rehearsal as if the teacher was in the room, we didn't slack off and we never showed up late just because we could.

    Those are the people you need to surround yourself with,

those that will encourage and push you. People who are committed, focused, and kind. It will do you no good to surround yourself with those who are slackers, unkind or those who come across as if they don't care. Even if it doesn't rub off on you, your peers will associate you with those type of people and may not trust you to work with them.

There was this one girl who I knew my first semester at AMDA who would join Jada and I during our study sessions and late-night rehearsals, she made steady progress every week, she ended up being in my group in a later semester, but she fell in with a different crowd, a crowd that slacked, prioritized having a good time over the work and were known for not really caring. It rubbed off on her and she wasn't the same girl I knew first semester. It's sad to see someone move backwards, but that proves just how much the people you surround yourself with matter. It makes a difference, trust me.

Please find you a good solid crew who will benefit you in the long run. Don't fall in with the wrong crowd, it can be so tempting to have a good time all the time especially with the workload you have during training. Ask yourself this question, Is a good time every night for a few weeks more important to you than your career?

      Don't confuse finding your crew with forming a clique. Once you find your crew don't close yourself to other friendships within your classes or groups. Don't be a mean girl and cast people out. You should still seek friendships with those outside your set crew if you like them. Even if you don't like them don't make them feel as if you and your friends are cliqued up against them. You and your friends should not be judging others while they work, whispering about others during class, exchanging looks that indicate your judgmental thoughts or secretively snickering. This is a safe space for everyone to work, grow and make mistakes, your peers shouldn't feel ashamed to do so because of you being judgmental with your clique.

If you do find yourself wanting to judge and bad mouth others (It's college, it happens, I understand) please don't do it where the work happens. That is just disrespectful. Save it for another time and place.

An Actor In Training

"Soak it all in, enjoy this moment of doing what you love every single day for the weeks, months or even years you are in your training. I had absolutely no training, or theatre experience before I started my training. I came into it blind yet excited to do what I love every day, No one was there to hold my hand, I had to make sure I was on top of my game from the very beginning.

Make sure you are self-disciplined. Training can get the best of you if you are ill prepared. Set yourself up for success with managing your time properly, putting in the extra hours, dedicating yourself to the work while you have the opportunity.

I love the whole structure of training programs, the discipline they require and having the opportunity to literally act 24/7. It should be looked at as a privilege to do this every day. Not saying it doesn't become tough some days, but those are the days when it really counts to be dedicated and have good work ethic.

You meet so many wonderful people while in training, sometimes even lifelong friends, or people you will work with in the near future so it's very important to not only be kind to everyone but to set a standard that everyone can remember. You never know where anyone is going to end up in this industry.

Remember why you wanted to do this in the first place, keep that same love, passion and drive you had in the beginning with you throughout your training and I promise it will be magical every day."

-Nadia Brown

Actress/Model

Nadia is an actress based in New York City. She is currently Rose Granger-Weasley in Harry Potter and the Cursed Child on Broadway. Nadia has trained at the Royal Academy of Dramatic Art in London, UK., the British American Drama Academy at Oxford University and graduated Summa Cum Laude from Marymount Manhattan College

Javaris Tip #8
Know what's going on

It's important to become acclimated with the school you are attending and know what's going on. If there are any clubs or student groups you may be interested in joining, any fun activities happening that week to see If there are any special events going on such as extra dance classes, panels or guest speakers coming in soon. AMDA offered Strength and conditioning class once or twice a week which was my favorite! A big perk of AMDA was that we got free tickets to Broadway

An Actor In Training

shows! Oh how I miss those free tickets!

Be Your own Biggest Fan

It's important to be your own biggest fan from the very beginning. You are going to be entering a world where everyone around you is incredibly talented and skilled. It can be intimidating at first being around so many strong performers with big personalities. I was especially taken back by this my first few weeks in training. I had no prior theatre experience, and I never had the opportunity to work with other actors before. I felt as if I didn't belong, that everyone else around me was so much better than I was, I felt as if I didn't know anything and that I was the weakest link. It turns out that almost everyone in my group felt the same way about themselves and put everyone else on a pedestal. I realized that I wasn't alone. We all came to terms with ourselves, our talent and skills and we weren't as hard on ourselves later. You must remind yourself that you are talented, skilled, you have something to offer, and you are a star! Don't forget to pair all that self-discipline with some self-love.

Your Teachers Are Not Your cheerleaders

Many people come into their training expecting their teachers to praise them and give them compliments around the clock, well that's not how this works. You will quickly realize that your teachers are not there to be your cheerleaders. You honestly shouldn't expect any praise whatsoever, besides the occasional "Great Work". If you are seeking compliments and praise for your work in training, you are in the wrong place. A wise teacher of mine told me "If I focused on everything you were doing right, we'd be here all night.

I remember I got a note once to change my stance in a scene, it was too narrow for the circumstances of the scene. We worked on the scene for weeks and I never got confirmation if my new stance was good or not. One day the teachers says, "I gave Javaris the note to fix his stance and he did, and I've never had to bring it up again". If a teacher does not say anything about a previous note, you most likely corrected whatever it was.

You should never ask the teacher for any notes if there were none given initially. If they had something to say, they would have said it. You should be happy when you receive no notes. During my final showcase for AMDA one of my directors began giving notes to the cast and she points at me and says "Javaris, I have no notes for you tonight". You better believe I was floating on a cloud home that night.

Opinions Are Opinions

Everyone has opinions about everything, even things that don't concern them. You will encounter those who feel the need to share their opinions about other people's work or even your work, and most of the time it's somewhat negative. Be cautious of these people. If they feel so free to share their negative opinions about someone else's work to you, they can do the same thing about your work to someone else. You can have your opinions of course, but as I said earlier in the book, be careful of who to share them with.

An Actor In Training

When someone has an opinion about your work and they decide to share it without you asking, it can be Jarring. Who the hell do you think you are? Meryl Streep? Nothing grinds my gears more than someone who thinks they can tell me about my work without me asking. It's not okay and please don't be one of those people. I had this one classmate who would take it upon himself to give my friends and me notes while having lunch. It became so annoying that one day I told him, that he isn't the director and should stop trying to give us notes because it killed the vibe every time. No one likes unsolicited opinions on their work, especially when it's something so precious as our art.

Don't take anything Personally

You are going to hear it a million times in your training and in this industry. DO NOT take anything personally. Any notes that you are being given, any constructive criticism or feedback of any kind are to help you grow as an artist, they are not to personally attack you or your talent. People do themselves a disservice when they begin to take things personally. They begin to close themselves off from the work and that can cause major issues. If a teacher tells you that a certain role may not be right for you don't take it personally and think it's because you aren't "good enough" it can be quite the opposite.

I remember telling one of my directors for my final showcase that I loved the character Puck from "A Midsummer Night's Dream" by William Shakespeare and that I'd love to pitch it for showcase. She told me that although she loves that play and puck himself, she saw me more heroic and romantic and felt I'd be better suited in a role such as Lysander or even Duke Orsino from "Twelfth Night" by William Shakespeare. Well, she was right, I pitched twelfth night and was cast as Duke Orsino, and it was the most fun I'd had with a role in a long time.

That's the way this industry works, and they are only trying to prepare you for the real world once you leave your training and begin to audition. Please don't take anything personal or you will end up doing more harm to yourself than good.

Take Care Of Yourself

Training can be rigorous, challenging and exhausting. It is imperative that you take care of yourself during your time there, both physically and mentally. Taking care of myself physically

An Actor In Training

came second nature to me and I had no issue with that however it took me a long time to navigate how to take care of myself mentally while in training, ultimately causing me to burnout.

Taking care of yourself physically can be anything that's going to help condition you instrument. You are using your body every single day for hours on end, it can be challenging if you are not properly taking care of your instrument, you can even injure yourself if you aren't careful. For some people it may look like doing yoga every day before or after class, for others it may be massage guns or even just lying in bed after a long day before continuing with their workload. For me it was working out every day, eating as healthy as I could on a college budget and stretching each morning. Everyone is different and I can't tell you what will work for your body, so feel free to explore things that may aid you physically during your time in training.

It is just as important if not more, to take care of yourself mentally while in training. This road isn't an easy one to travel, A lot is going to be thrown at you, you are going to have extreme workloads at some points, and it can all be overwhelming at times. Having some type of system in place to take care of yourself mentally will help you tremendously. It can be anything that gives you that brain break that we all need every now and then, like going for a walk, meditating, sitting in a room alone with good music, watching an episode of your favorite TV show for an hour or even just sitting to chat with some good friends. Whatever you feel is best for you.

It can be hard navigating this, especially when you're someone like me who doesn't know when to take a break sometimes. I remember during my second semester I worked myself until the wheels almost fell off, not taking any time for myself, Working around the clock like a maniac. Yes, it's important to have a good work ethic but not to the point where it's causing you to burnout. All my friends kept saying I looked like I was burning out, but I denied it saying I was just more focused than ever. Well, they were right, I crashed and burned hard. Luckily it was around a holiday break, so I had time to recoup before returning to classes.

    Fortunately, AMDA has on campus mental health counselors who are free to utilize as much as you'd like. Check to see if your school offers any mental health counseling services in case you choose to utilize them.

Please take care of yourself because no one else is. It's going to aid you in the long run, I promise. Take a step back after your first few weeks in training and check in with yourself, ask yourself are you okay, ask if you are taking care of yourself properly. Love yourself.

"Your self-confidence is going to waver in this business. What you must realize is everyone is on their own path. If you find yourself comparing yourself to others, your self-confidence is going to plummet.

Control what's in your power, you can't control casting or what people think of you, but you can control your attitude and work ethic and that is noticed. People love to work with people who are kind and hard workers.

I cannot stress how important it is to have something else you love to do in your life. Whether you are going to a university or you're in a conservatory studying theatre 24/7, make sure you have dedicated time for other things that will serve you well.

Be mindful of who you surround yourself with. The people around you can build you up or tear you down quickly. Also be mindful of your classmates and teachers, they could be the ones granting you job opportunities years down the line. You never know where a connection may lead you down the line

Say yes as much as possible, say yes to a role that challenges you, say yes to a class that scares you, say yes to getting coffee with someone that may change your entire life. You never know where a yes can take you."

-Maggie Bera
Actress

Maggie is the creator and host of the "Actor Aesthetic" podcast. Off-Broadway, Maggie appeared in *The Baker's Wife* at Theatre Row (working alongside original composer Stephen Schwartz) and originated the role of Ruby in *Helen on 86th St.* at the Chernuchin Theatre.

Javaris Tip #9
Keep A Journal

Keeping a journal during my training was my saving grace at times.

I recommend always keeping a journal on you, both in and out of class. Of course, you know to have one to write all your notes, blocking and general feedback in but it's very helpful to have one that you write your personal feelings in. We are expected to be more vulnerable than most students during our training so keeping in touch with how you feel through journaling can keep you in tune with yourself.

That's a wrap!

I hope this book has given you some good advice and serves you well. I want you to take what you've learned from this book and apply it to your everyday life during your time in training.

You are the catalyst for everything great in your life. You have the power to make your time in training and amazing experience you'll treasure for life or one of the worst things you've ever done in your life.

When you begin your training, you are entering a new world. A world where you have the chance to reinvent yourself. No on knows your past. This is an

An Actor In Training

opportunity to create a whole new you. The you that you've always wanted to be. A version of yourself that embodies everything you've ever wanted.

If you take nothing else from this book, please take the fact that hard work, perseverance, and a good attitude will take you further than you could have ever imagined

Use the information in this book wisely. It is not to be used to try and compete against others. It is not to give you a big head or inflate your ego. It is to aid you in your training. Allowing you to pass the information along to you friends.

An Actor In Training

Please be patient, respectful and kind to everyone, and yourself!

I think the only appropriate way to end this book would be with a quote from the great man himself.

    I leave you with this

"Some are born great; some achieve greatness, and some have greatness thrust upon them."

Acknowledgments

Special Thanks to.

Dave Shalansky,

Ray Virta,

Suzy Jane Hunt,

America Barcenas De La Luz

Nadia Brown,

And Maggie Bera.

An Actor In Training